THE PROBABLE HURDLES IN THE CAMEROON 2035 DREAM

By

Kelly NGYAH

I0102278

Research & Working Papers Initiative towards Global Peace and Development @ MAHSRA publications
2014

Content

Abstract

O Cameroon, Thou Cradle of our
Fathers…….

………….Thy welfare we will win in
toil and love and peace,

………………………..Will be to thy
name ever true!

Land of Promise, land of Glory!

Thou, of life and joy, our only store!

Thine be honour, thine devotion,

And deep endearment, for evermore.

And so a nation, was born upon the cradle of
our four fathers,

Within the fundamental principles of love and
peace, this nation ate its first fruits, made its
first steps, and solemnized itself with the
values of truth and stability;

Enclosed within the ethical realms of pride and self-confident abilities, the nation endowed its soil with the promise of a venerated prosperity and an honoured affluence;

Destined to be extolled for bringing social harmony and solidarity amongst all its progeny, the nation's affectionate future has been engraved by faith and eternal devout.

Introduction

Cameroon is a country endowed with so much and so diverse resources but yet very little to show for its abundance. History had its part to play in the development of the present day politics but so much of this history has not been the major concern of the subjects within such a great nation. The present ambitions of the country are huge but the present political and socioeconomic situation of the country, though virtually reflective as dependable, yet the objectivist reality is actually appalling. Is there something wrong somewhere that both its citizens and third party observers can't see?

Given that the big ambitious vision of the nation in becoming an emerging nation by 2035 seems to be vigorously active and on its way, another pertinent worry is that the country has been analyzed and alleged to be a' fragile state' liable to fall into a severe civil disorder soonest.

In the attempt to cross examine these suspicions; this study has infiltrated certain historical grievance factors as far back as the country's pre-historic literature holds through its pre-colonial, colonial and post colonial existence and determined the probably elements that may or may not be liable to reactivate the old-wounds used for classifying country as 'fragile state'.

From an objectivist perspective, one would neither say the alleged fragility of the state may lead to a conflict or not, but for the sake of peace and stability, the study infiltrates the countries ambitious development vision and proposes firm peace institution stances within such that its citizenry may be perfectly apt for counteracting any major conflict issues or crises.

The Country Cameroon

From An Administrative Corner

Situated along the lines of West and Central Africa, Cameroon is a multiparty presidential regime (official legalization for multiparty politics —1960). Endorsed as the United Republic of Cameroon through Law No. 84-1 of 4 February 1984[1], the country's State power is exercised by the president of the republic and parliament meanwhile the judiciary power which is independent of the executive and legislative is coordinated through the supreme court, the court of appeal and tribunals exercising their authorities within stated territorial administrative partitions of the country and according to a dual legal or law application systems— English common law and the French civil law. The dual law application system within

---

[1] See the 1996 constitution of Cameroon.

the country stems from the fact that during the colonial period, the present day Cameroon was formerly as by the UN trusteeship territory mandates, administered by different countries using different legal systems. When both territories became united as federated entities via the UN sponsored plebiscite[2] on the 11th of February 1961—the southern Cameroons gained their independence by agreeing to merge with the French La République du Cameroon, both systems of law became applicable to the united territories.

Since the 11th February merger initiative, Cameroon has generally enjoyed a virtual stability which has permitted the critical development of agriculture, roads, and railways, as well as a petroleum industry though there has been several criticisms that despite its democratic movement toward democratic reform within obviously

---

[2] See International Crisis Group (2010: 32).

flawed democratic practices, political power remains firmly in the hands of an ethnic oligarchy. To facilitate the central administrative control over the territorial limits of the country, the central administration in the attempt to show-case its moves towards contemporary democratic reforms, instituted a highly passive decentralization mechanism. This is obviously a docile system comparatively with deconcentrated authorities who exercise direct delegated central power over the decentralized collectivities. Partitioned through 10regions, 58divisions and 370subdivisions, all territorial administrative units are drafted in such a way to be under the central administration's direct influence and control. This works even for the least local decentralized municipality or traditional entity — through appointed regional governors, divisional officers, government delegates and sub-divisional officers.

Figure 1. *Administrative map of Cameroon*

Evolutionary scope of the Cameroons' Economy

From an economical perspective, because of its oil resources and favorable agricultural conditions, Cameroon has one of the best-endowed primary commodity economies in sub-Saharan Africa. But its major economical problem began with its economic crises from the mid-1980s to the early 2000s which resulted in rising prices in Cameroon, trade deficits, and loss of government revenue. After acknowledging the crises in 1987 and being blamed by the outside observers and critics for poor government stewardship of the economy, the government instead placed the blame on the fall of the prices of export commodities, particularly a steep drop in the price of petroleum.[3]

In another perspective, the introductory democratization process of the early 1990s

[3] See DeLancey, Mark W., and Mark Dike DeLancey (2000: 104).

unfortunately occurred in a period of severe economic crisis having an outcome in 1993 that got the State close to bankruptcy and was forced to slash civil service pay (salaries) by 50 and 70 percent—which still, in a worsened instant had engraved effects from the inflationary devaluation of the CFA franc in 1994. Cameroonians still remember these measures with much contempt against the present regime and the International Monetary Fund (IMF) which some Cameroonians consider to have imposed the measures. Even though the economy recovered in the late 90s, at least in terms of State finances, the situation of the victimized civil service personnel did not have any significant change and the continued problems of economic management have produced a relatively low 4% annual growth since 2000. Cameroon remains dependent on agricultural and mineral resources, with oil revenues constituting around a third of the government's revenues.[4]

The country's problems are as severe as those faced by other underdeveloped countries, such as a top-heavy civil service and a generally unfavorable climate for business enterprise. From1990, the government has embarked on various IMF and World Bank programs designed to spur business investment, increase efficiency in agriculture, improve trade, and recapitalize the nation's banks. Since then, the government had been focused on paying off its international debt and further restricting public salaries and pay rises to civil servants.[5] In June 2000, the government completed an IMF-sponsored, three-year structural adjustment program; however, the IMF is pressing for more reforms, including increased budget transparency, privatization, and poverty reduction programs.

---

[4] See Célestin Monga (2009); Florence Charlier and Charles N'Cho- Oguie (2009).

[5] DeLancey et al. op ct. 105

Amidst the country's long bumpy economy pathway, some recent analyses show that there is still hope for the country's economic development expectations. According to the World Bank's Cameroon Economic Update produced bi-annually which analyzes trends and constraints on recent economic developments in the country and with aims to share knowledge and stimulate debate among those interested in improving the economic management of Cameroon and unleashing its enormous potential, it writes that:

> Despite increased economic growth, poverty rates in the West African nation of Cameroon have not declined, according to the latest Cameroon Economic Update, in the country's poorest

regions, poverty and hunger
continue to rise. [6]

This implies that the economic wealth of the country is truly under the manipulative calculations of a few who care very little or not at all about the wellbeing of the entire nation. 'The economic burden posed by the ministry of finance through wrongful award of contracts, extortion from foreign investors, mismanagement, customs and fiscal fraud is worse today than in 1982'[7]. The impasses for local development at the profit of the poor and vulnerable populations seem obviously to be coming from the core of the nations' economic power—bribery and fraud within the ministry of finance. How can the poverty crises within the poor regions thereby be handled to equate living standards like the economic growth

---

[6] See Raju Singh (2013).

[7] See Tiendi J. Ngalim (2006).

rate that is earmarked by the World Bank report?
Still according to the Cameroon update,

> the fifth in the series, titled
> Mitigating   Poverty,
> Vulnerability, and Risk, too
> few resources are being put
> into   small-scale,   ad   hoc
> social safety net programs,
> programs meant to improve
> the   lives   of   the
> poor'—economic momentum
> observed in 2012 is expected
> to carry over into 2013 with
> the   construction   of   large
> infrastructure projects and
> continued efforts to improve
> agricultural productivity. [8]

As convivially convincing as the report may
sound to the external world, one still wonders if it

---

[8] See Raju Singh (2013).

is not the usual rhetoric concocted and/or
manipulated by some of the depraved high
ranking government officials who are liable to get
involved or be discovered in the next multibillion
CFA francs embezzlement[9] of funds meant for
provision of local development support in poor
communities. The World Bank report further says
that the economic growth in Cameroon has on
average over the past decade, hovered around
three percent thus lagging behind the average oil-
exporting middle- and low- income countries in
sub-Saharan Africa which have experienced

---

[9] An exemplary situation of embezzlement is given at the
most recent September 21, 2012, Mfoundi High Court
ruling against Marafa Hamidou Yaya – former Secretary
General at the Presidency, Minister of State, Minister of
Territorial Administration and Decentralization and Yves
Michel Fotso – former Administrative Director of the
defunct Cameroonian Airlines (CAMAIR) accused as
principal persons involved in the embezzlement scam of
close to 31billion F.CFA that was set aside by the
Cameroon Hydrocarbon company, SNH for the acquisition
of the presidential plane. *Found in Page 8 of the
CHRONICLE newspaper, N° 323 of September 17 – 23,
2012.*

expansions of about 7.5 percent. This is an actual astonishing national qualification in which instead of getting results of better living standards for the people, the country still hosts several unemployed populations lamenting on the streets on daily basis in search of survival opportunities. Furthermore, because the World Bank's update is categorically emphatic on the fact that in contrast to other countries' economic activities in 2012, economic growth in Cameroon as well as other sub-Saharan countries has continued to gain momentum. This is gotten via preliminary indications which suggest that economic growth rate could reach about 5 percent in 2012, as compared to 4.2 percent in 2011.[10] The base line within this virtual analysis is that, while many people's living standards have become precarious, others have continued to accumulate what appears to be fabulous wealth, usually surrounded by suspicions

---

[10] See Raju Singh (2013).

of political connections and are surely the only ones who benefit from this economic growth. This has caused growing resentment and a perception that the social glue built up under Ahidjo has weakened. President Biya himself has said: 'I believe that a society running at several different speeds, as well as moving away from our traditional customs of solidarity, would quickly lose cohesion and become subject to serious internal tensions'.[11]

However, the recent progress of the country with regards its economy appreciation is worth acclaiming, but other major worries still tilt towards the apparent political stability of the country. In an international crises group report, it writes that:

> Cameroon's   apparent
> stability in a turbulent region
> cannot be taken for granted.

---

[11] See Bouopda Pierre Kamé (2008).

The co-option of elites
through the distribution of
state largesse, and the
emigration of many educated
young people provide a
certain safety valve for
tensions, but the failure of
reform and continued poor
governance mean people no
longer believe in the rule of
law or peaceful political
change. Multiple risks of
conflict exist in the build-up
to presidential elections in
2011 and beyond.[12]

In producing this research work, my fear
runs along that of the probable conflict
expectancy analysis produced by the international
Crises Group. This is because if a major outbreak

---

[12] See International Crisis Group (2010: i).

of civil war occurs in a country that has never experienced nor controlled such hostilities before, the country may become very vulnerable to external spoilers' maneuvers and as such help in bringing its own long construed economy progress to nothing. Thus, a study of the historical facts that have always tilted the country towards probable major hostilities and the need to put in place highly strategized and institutionalized mechanisms to sustain the virtual peace situation and also effectively manage and eradicate conflict provocation or catalyst moves is necessary in order to maintain the development outcomes of the country and its future generations.

Cameroon's History of Conflicts

Due to recent revolutionary movements that have affected countries which seemed to have been fast developing under their authoritarian rulers along Africa and the Middle East, such as the 2011 Arab spring, a more critical school on conflict prognostic analysts have emerged and pertinent issues categorical to autocratic regimes in virtual stability within certain contemporary nation-States are now under question. Cameroon as one of the major targets presents the following situational findings:

- **Prehistoric Age**. The conflict history in Cameroon is reported to have begun in prehistoric times having the country's legacy of ethnic diversity that dates back to 8,000 BCE with the migration of the Baka people into the country's modern-day borders. It explains that by 200 BCE, an influx of Bantu-speaking tribes into the southern and eastern regions of the country had pushed the Bakas off arable land and into the nearby forests.[13] This

---

[13] See Pre-colonial History of Cameroon. Sourced online at: http://gci-cameroon.org/about-cameroon/history-of-cameroon/ . Accessed on the 24th of May 2013.

implicates the fact that some ethnic groups of the country had already begun sustaining grievances against their superior adversaries who forced them out of their rich and cultivable soils. Through such a lengthy period and for the fact that such grievances were based on livelihood resource denial for a community in need, the severity of the outcomes faced by the such a community forced to wander for survival in the forest, might have instilled and probably transmitted the consequences on a generational basis. The question here is where those grievances ever resolved?

• **The Pre-trusteeship colonial Era**. This period was characterized by the German's institution of Cameroon's economic geography through an obvious establishment of large plantations along the south coast of the country. The German economic development projects in Cameroon (then Called Kamerun) that spread over an approximated period of 35 years (from 1884 to 1919), strongly assisted in sharpening the ethnic differences of the already multi-complex ethnic structure existing in the country by then. Their infiltration into the interior Cameroonian territories was accompanied by conquerors battles that dismantled the strongholds of several tribal peoples[14] and their territories and also pushed African traders out of their previously lucrative intermediary positions. All of the early development battles came at a huge cost to the

---

[14] Ibid.

indigenous people of the country. From
the writings of a handful of researchers,
it is probable to link the pre-trusteeship
era to the pre-historic indigenous or
tribal peoples' grievances owing to the
fact that they all present occasions
where the livelihood land resources are
seized from the weak by powerful
groups. 'The Germans inflicted such
brutality that Governor Von Puttkamer
was recalled and disciplined, before a
supposedly more liberal colonial policy
was introduced in 1907'.[15] It is no
doubt that during such raiding
adventures of the Germans, they would
have been aided by rival ethnic groups
who desired to see their adversary
groups defeated and probably
eliminated. Thus, both interethnic

---

[15] See Richard Joseph(1977: 39-43); Victor T. Le Vine (1964
chap II); Achille Mbembe(1996: 44-68)

group grievances and the hatred for the
ferrous German administration might
have been critically nurtured. Have
these grievances been properly
addressed?

- **Cameroon under Trusteeship
  Mandate**. The first worries during this
  period were linked to the French's
  adoption and reinforcement of a public
  works' program. This was the colonial
  administration system that in
  economical terms highly speeded up
  the economic development of the
  country for over a 16years period
  (from1922 to 1938) but however, was
  implicatively prejudicial in the sense
  that it promoted forced labour against
  the mandate terms, and under the
  indigénat law[16], gave room for local

---

[16] See Victor T. Le Vine (1964: Chap IV); Richard

administrators to use the former unchecked powers over colonial subjects (involved instances of arbitrary beatings and whipping)[17]. On the part of the English, the major worry was in the neglectful attitude the protectorate administrators displayed towards the local indigenous land conflict problems that up till date is still a severe problem amongst some indigenous communities in the North West and South West regions of Cameroon[18] (regarded as southern Cameroons before the February 11, 1961 plebiscite). This third historical worry on the part of French Cameroon brings in a new element which is that

Joseph(1977: 43-56); Achille Mbembe(1996: Chap I and IV)

[17] See Thobie et al. (1990: chap 7)

[18] See Kelly F. NGYAH (2012a: 56-62)

of human rights violation of the indigenous populations especially with respect to the working classes then, but for the British Cameroons, conflicts over territorial land claims were predominant within the savanna zones. Also, the French and British Cameroons faced a similar up-growth of local political struggle when the local chieftaincies were reorganized by both the British and the French and graded according to importance (first to third degree chiefs).[19] And because this reorganisation did not only reinforced the role of previously accepted traditional authorities but created other chieftaincies in order manage the organization of labour and tax collection, a new dawn for power

---

[19] See Peter Geschiere(1993); Achille Mbembe(1996: Chap IV)

struggle towards obtaining these chieftaincy titles aroused—one of the first instances for indigenous conflicts for local political power. This lead to more vibrant indigenous political struggles for the post-colonial 'administrator-ship' posts over the labour and tax systems and also some corresponding passive moves towards independence especially during the Second World War which had a profound impact on the Cameroon's political development history. The World War 2 period weakened the colonial administrations because they had concentrated much of their efforts in battle prerequisites and obviously lessened their grip over the highly dependent indigenous populations. The results led to increased poverty levels which then brought about severe strike

actions and demonstrations in
September 1945 in Douala. Such were
met with force by the authorities, and
because the European colonizers also
developed fear of the already
minimally organized indigenous unions
and their activities in the new more
liberal post-war environment, they
formed ad hoc armed militias, which
killed several dozen demonstrators.[20]
As the struggles for local power to
access the then political chieftaincy
tittles for administrative benefits and
other selfish individualistic gains from
the colonial administration continued,
both British and French Cameroons
experienced vibrant political party
movements criticizing the protectorate
administrators and building momentum

---

[20] See Joseph, op. cit., chap II; and Achille, op. cit., chap VI.

towards an eventual fight for independence. In French Cameroun, Union des peuples du Cameroon, UPC Led by Ruben Um Nyobé, had quickly developed a radical nationalist platform, mobilising support against colonial abuses, especially in the south and west,[21] and had successfully articulated a nationalist agenda. This involved producing several regular newspapers and many political tracts and also sending tens of thousands of petitions to the point that France was not living up to commitments of the trusteeship agreement as in ending force labour and guiding the country towards its independence but was rather seeking to integrate it further into French colonial structures. In

---

[21] See Ibid Chap VI and VII; and Chap VII and VIII

British Cameroon, Emmanuel Endeley
and John Foncha were instrumental
figures behind the embryonic political
parties in the late 1940s—Kamerun
National Congress (KNC) and
Kamerun National Democratic Party
(KNDP) in 1955, and influential for the
autonomy battle for British Cameroon
within the Nigerian federation in the
Eastern Regional House of Assembly
and also served as the igniters for the
initial conceptive views of
reunification with French Cameroon in
order to pressurize British authorities to
see the further need of their regional
autonomy.[22] Another fact to discern
from the period in which both

---

[22] See Le Vine, op. cit., chap.VIII; Nicodemus F.
Awasom(1998);

Piet Konings and Francis Nyamnjoh (2003: chap. 2); and
Jean-François Bayart (1979: 110-117)

Cameroons were under trusteeship is that, from the old struggle over territorial claims, issues had only mutated to a more meaningful autonomy and/or political control over such ideals. The people never wanted to be under control of both foreign or an unreasonable[23] local rule.

- **The Advent of Independence**. This period was characterized by massive violence for the expression of the true Cameroonian political person or citizenry—explained above as an auto-cognitive liberal citizen. It followed that in 1954, the new governor's Roland Pré mission which was to cramp down the activities of liberalist and nationalist movement motives of

---

[23] Unreasonable means: a dictatorial government system wherein their values and positions are of limited or no importance.

UPC, on the contrary worsen the crises situation at the time. In his attempt to unite efforts with some conservative indigenous leaders unions and distort UPC's goals, the UPC militants became excessively furious and aggressive—partly, I believe because they would not stand to see a foreigner turn their indigenous brothers against them and on the other hand because they thought the freedom of Cameroonians would not be decided by the same rule that was suppose to guide them towards their independence and not impose their own system on them. As such, in 1955 wide spread riots were notice across the South West with road blocks and properties of pro-administration elites looted or destroyed. The violence culminated in running battles on the streets of Douala during the last days of May, pitting the army (including reinforcements from neighbouring French colonies) against UPC militants and unionists—worth noting here is the fact that these riots have been compared to other recent struggles such as that of February 2008.[24] After blaming and banning UPC from political elections because of riots, the true and free minded Cameroonian personality as of the nature of the UPC militants, fought against such a discriminating decision. This via an ill prepared guerilla war, lead to the UN's intervention at a later date and was also consequential to the death of Um Nyombé in September 1958. For the fact that the death of Um Nyombé greatly weakened the

[24] See Joseph, op. cit., chap VIII and IX and Mbembe, op. cit., pp. 319-327.

movement, one would wonder if such
paralyses are not only temporal and
may arise again in the future based on
*nurtured grievances of his 'maybe new
generation followers'*. In French
Cameroon, the advent of independence
was a flawed process because the
totality or majorities of the indigenous
leaders of Cameroun citizens were not
in accord—In fact, the main authors for
the independence were not involved. It
follows that, meanwhile UPC (the
major nationalist party) was passively
active in exile, Ahidjo whom I would
consider a treacherous ally with de
Gaulle[25] was able to manipulate the

---

[25] I have considered Ahidjo as treacherous because As a
deputy to Mbida the prime minister at the head of a
heterogeneous coalition, he was suppose to be supportive
of ideologies in the interest of his indigenous people but it
is given that: .... de Gaulle's return to power in 1958 and
the consequent rapid changes across French colonial Africa.
Mbida, whose changes of position on the question of

calls for a national conference on the
fate of the post-colonial Cameroun by
using the insurgency as a pretext to
declare a state of emergency and then
take full executive powers for himself.
As such, he obtained independence in
January 1961 without any general
consensus—thus leading to the
promulgation of a constitution modeled
by his French allies. With this stance,
another question that one may pose is
that, did French Cameroon actually
gain its independence from an
objectivist perspective that merits the
authentication of moral ethics? If not,

---

independence were notorious, proved unable to keep his
coalition together and was forced from office in February
1958. He was replaced by Ahidjo, who had cleverly
distanced himself from Mbida several months before and
had maintained close relations with the French authorities,
who retained the power to name the prime minister. See
Bayart, op. cit., chap I; and victor Le Vine, op. cit., chapter
VII.

then we have another course to worry about the *probability of a nationalist objectivists' conflict in the making.* In British Cameroon, the 1959 legislative elections that led to the change of the post of the prime minister from Endeley to Foncha, marked another flawed independence movement process. In contrast to the Adamou Ahidjo who was aware of his treacherous complicity, Foncha seemed to be a non-optimist and individualists visionary leader who not only thought of his self-centered pleasure in pressurizing and building his importance at the face of the British protectorate administrators but was also very carefree about the actual needs and Anglophone heritage attachments that the southern Cameroonians had with their neigbouring former British colony Nigeria.[26] Though the intentions of Foncha were that of a true Cameroonian spirit in a struggle for autonomy and his position might probably have been influenced by the lofty negotiations with Ahidjo who was obviously supported by the French, his hasty decision for the referendum in support for the partially consolidate constitutional union with French Cameroun proves his weakened and self-centered visionary mind given that there were almost no solid guarantees to enact what was to be, on paper, a 'union of equal parts'. The resulting frustrations linger today in Anglophone Cameroon.[27] A more very prominent

---

[26] See Konings and Nyamnjoh, op. cit., chap. 2; and Awasom, op. cit.
[27] Ibid.

aspect to note between the French and English Cameroonian citizenship dilemma is that the country's pre and post colonial leadership misguidance have grown in them a spirit of lack of faith in public institutions and the prevalent understanding that the rules of the game are ultimately contingent on political power.

- **Post independent Cameroon under Ahidjo**. After independence, we begin to assess more measures and instances through which the Cameroonian people have been either denied their rights to liberal and free participation in the political affairs of their country or manipulated into submerging their original liberal aspirations under Ahidjo's rule. This follows that, after his accession into power, by gradually picking off members of opposition parties through offers of government positions and developing his idea of a 'national unified party' as the only way to counter the dangers of fragmentation, he moved step by step towards the single-party state and with the strong advantages of presidential patronage, his party became an efficient machine for gathering elite support.[28] Also, early 1962, when a group of four oppositions (Charles Bebey Eyidi, Théodore Mayi Matip, mbida and Okala) censured that Ahidjo was trying to install an autocratic rule and called for a broad opposition front, he arrested and jailed all of them. Yet, there was however still a significant

---

[28] See Bayart (1978); Victor Le Vine Le Vine, op. cit., chap IX; Konings and Nyamnjoh, op. cit., pp. 2-9; M.W. Delancey (1987); and Jean-François Médard (1978)

opposition support from some UPC
elites who continued violence around
Bafoussam. The violence was intended
to provoke a delicate balance between
mobilising their base, which remained
strongly opposed to Ahidjo's
government, and demonstrating their
ability to be a serious legal political
party.[29] In the then Western Cameroon
in which Foncha had automatically
gain the position of a federated entity
president as it was seeming ('in line
with constitutional changes, Foncha
had to give up one or the other post in
1965. He chose to remain federal vice
president'.[30]), his absence as a result of
his federal duties, lead to the split of

---

[29] See Dominique Malaquais (2002: chap 5); M. Terretta
(2005)

[30] See footnote (23) in International Crises Group (2010: 8)

the political stability and party system within the zone. Partly supported by Ahidjo, this was obviously a move to bring disorder and to totally consolidate Ahidjo's grip over the former Southern Cameroons—the distorted and defragmented parties later joined the Cameroonian National Union (CNU) as the only legal political movement proposed by Ahidjo. Later, through a centralized and systemic political manipulation of a government services and ministries' controlled from the presidential office in Yaounde and under a single legal political movement that granted 22 seats for the eight Anglophone parties, a federated entity silently lost its autonomy to the egoistic Unitarian mercy of the other. The *impacts of such a manipulation over a whole people, is not without*

*great consequences that should be left
unaddresse*d. In a further instant, the
disrespect and disregard showered onto
the West Cameroon's federated entity
as in administering it in a similar way
as one of the French Cameroun's then
instituted provinces (East Cameroun's
five provinces), is said to have been a
major source of frequent clashes
between the elected Anglophone
officials and the staff of the federal
administrators sent from Yaoundé. It is
also acknowledged that, tensions
became particularly acute because of
the security forces' petty abuses of
power (Francophone gendarmes, who
were all under federal authority) —a
stance that up till date still remains a
source of bitterness in Anglophone
Cameroon.[31]

- **Post independent Cameroon after Adhijo**. As Ahidjo resigned from the presidential seat due to illness, the major challenges in the country then as his technocratic successor took over was in managing on the one hand, the centralized clientelist system he and his supporters inherited from Ahidjo and have maintained, on the other, the contemporary prerequisites for an open debate, choice and popular legitimacy that have periodically emerged irrespective of whether in the one-party state or within a pluralist setting. Biya's ambitions then took a more uniformist and modernist approach which was undeniably innovative to the Cameroonian system—referred to as 'the renewal' (*le renouveau*) –

[31] The Southern Cameroon's National Council (SCNC) supporters explain in an interview October 2011

combined with much talk of combating
corruption (*rigueur*), welcomed by
many and gave in one of the more
reasons why he was later voted as the
legitimate president under a non-
competitive elections. Some of his
technocratic endeavors to win popular
opinion also included some regime
opponents, who came back from exile
in the course of 1983 and 1984.[32]

- **Cameroon Faces New Challenges in
  the Advent of Democratization**. The
  period of the real Cameroonian
  citizenry aspirations had come, and this
  was another moment in Cameroon
  history that brought so much
  disappointments and grievances upon
  the people against their governing

---

[32] See footnote (40) in International Crises Group
(2010: 11)

system. It followed that, one of the first victims to the movement was lawyer Yondo Black who attempted to form a new political party early in 1990 but was arrested along with a dozen other democracy activists.[33]This resulted to a strike action led by Bernard Muna and some UPC militants. In the next instance, the foundation meeting of the Social Democratic Front (SDF) by John Fru Ndi was violently put down by the army, at the cost of six civilian lives.[34] In a later instant, foreign inspirations on the democratic tendencies in the form of a national

---

[33] See footnote (46): Characteristic of Cameroon's conflicting legal provisions, this was his right under the constitution, but illegal according to the 1967 anti-sedition laws. International Crises Group (2010:12) .

[34] See Milton Krieger (2008: chap 2). *Cameroon's Social Democratic Front: Its History and Prospects as an Opposition Party (1990-2011)* (Bamenda, 2008)

conference gripped the Cameroonian people demanding for same and which was obviously denied by the current regime—the refusal built anger and tension amongst the people and led to the arrest of some journalists and opposition parties and civil society groups (such as CAP liberté, led by Djeukam Tchamani) who organised a general strike and 'ghost towns movement, intended to shut down the economy and put pressure on a government that wouldn't yield in.[35] After negotiations and promises which yielded at holding a precipitous legislative elections at the beginning of March 1992— the opposition obviously boycotted the elections[36]

---

[35] See International Crises Group (2010:12)

[36] See Joseph Takougang (1996).

because they deemed it to abrupt and needed time to prepare, but the technocratic regime however still skillfully induce other pressure-centered convincing models by offering huge sums of money to those parties who agree to participate. Human greed however played to the favour of the technocrats as they saw the dawn of major opposition party fragmentations between the militants who would prefer to take the money and participate and those who stood by their values—This particular instant is a predominant oligarchic situation faced in Cameroon today with the present ruling party which uses money and other lucrative livelihood sustenance opportunities to win over the support from its militants. During the October 1992 presidential elections, tensions were already high after a violent campaign fuelled by the regime's blatant attempts to manipulate the vote—International observers reported "serious flaws" in the electoral process.[37] The real uprising came on October 23rd when the Supreme announced president Biya's victory—it sparked an outrage of very ugly riots in which disappointed youths and delinquents got involved in the mob destructionist activism within Bamenda—burning down the houses of all pronounced CPDM supporters and even to the extreme of roasting some persons alive like the late Fomukong Tita who was a great CPDM supporter

---

[37] See footnote (51) See "An Assessment of the October 11, 1992 Election in Cameroon", National Democratic Institute for International Affairs, Washington, 1993. International Crises Group (2010: 13)

in Bamenda at the time. Biya imposed
a state of emergency rule in the then
Northwest Province, and the military
came down hard on the city.[38] In the
following years after the presidential
and legislative elections in 1997
granted 43 seats out of 180 to SDF.
However, the democratic advances of
the country became short-lived as the
CPDM learned to use the advantages of
incumbency more effectively (through
the exploitation of its full regime
powers via harassment of independent
media, selective distribution of state
resources, highly partisan
administration as well as fraud and
manipulation at ball points in the

---

[38] See See "Arrests after emergency rule in Cameroon
province", Reuters, 28 October 1992; "Riots in Cameroon
after President Biya re-elected", Reuters, 23 October 1992;
and Ngoh, in John Mukum Mbaku and Joseph Takougang
(eds.) (2004: 442).

electoral process)[39] to restore authoritarian rule, pushing the opposition back to small ethno-regional enclaves in the 2002 elections. This stance is translated through an assessment of the dying hopes of the Cameroonian people in the democratization process within the country perceived in the lack of credibility in elections and the current very low voter registration rates which were both blocking maneuvers of the regime and a growing popular disenchantment.[40]

The long historical line of instituted hurdles that have actually been accessed to be the root causes of the Cameroonian people's passive

---

[39] See footnote (57): A Crisis Group researcher was an electoral observer in Douala in 2002 and witnessed these problems first hand. International Crises Group (2010: 15)

[40] Idid See footnote (58)

but very intense grievances cannot be exhausted
without screening its most recent diabolic
manifestation of corrupt government officials.

Corruption and the Cameroonian People

Ranging from No. 1 out of 85 in 1998 up
tonNo. 144 out of 176 in 2012 of the world's most
corrupt country according to transparency
international, one may be forced to imply that
Cameroon has made a considerable interest in the
fight against corruption, yet in recent times the
news of public officials being jailed over the
embezzlement of several billions of F.CFA comes
on regular bases[41]. The exorbitant sums of State

---

[41] For instance, as concerns financial fluxes gathered by the
Unit for Financial Investigation in Cameroon, 40 files had
been transmitted to the courts during the 2011 financial
year amounting to FCFA 10,518,533,171(ten billion five
hundred and eighteen million five hundred and thirty three
thousand one hundred and seventy one francs). See
CONAC Publishes 2011 Corruption Report, Available on line
at: http://www.modernghana.com/news/433629/1/conac-
publishes-2011-corruption-report.html Retrieved on the
26th of May 2013; see also, Mfoundi High Court ruling of
the September 21, 2012 against Marafa Hamidou Yaya –

funds which are being siphoned from the state coffers into individual accounts, if calculated appropriately for a period of over 3years, it may amount to the desired funds required to institute and managed a highly strategized poverty eradication scheme that could significantly and permanently eliminate the higher poverty levels in all the vulnerable and less privileged communities within the territorial limits of the country. With this knowledge, there is no more wonder why though currently the World Bank's update has been categorically emphatic on the fact that in contrast to other countries' economic activities in 2012, economic growth in Cameroon has

---

former Secretary General at the Presidency, Minister of State, Minister of Territorial Administration and Decentralization and Yves Michel Fotso – former Administrative Director of the defunct Cameroonian Airlines (CAMAIR) accused as principal persons involved in the embezzlement scam of close to 31billion F.CFA that was set aside by the Cameroon Hydrocarbon company, SNH for the acquisition of the presidential plane. *Found in Page 8 of the CHRONICLE newspaper, Nº 323 of September 17 – 23, 2012; and many others*

continued to gain momentum with preliminary indications suggesting that economic growth could reach about 5 percent in 2012, as compared to 4.2 percent in 2011[42] but yet, despite increased economic growth, poverty rates in Cameroon have not declined and in the country's poorest regions, poverty and hunger continue to rise. [43] Meanwhile the government is absolutely making efforts to increase the development rate of the country and probably better the livelihood standards for some of its vulnerable populations, a few of its representatives with their solipsist mind frames do not see the later as an option and prefer to diabolically steal such huge sums of money meanwhile the majority of the population stays lavishing in abject poverty.

Corruption is an enemy to development and it harms the poor more than the others, stifles

---

[42] See Raju Singh (2013).

[43] See Raju Singh (2013).

economic growth and diverts desperately needed
funds from education, healthcare and other public
services. The Executive Director of the United
Nations Office on Drugs and Crime (UNODC),
Yury Fedotov had said that 'Corruption is a global
threat. It is a serious roadblock to economic
development,' — 'Corruption aggravates
inequality and injustice, and undermines stability,
especially in the world's most vulnerable regions.'[44]
The impact of corruption upon the economic
development in Cameroon is no doubt one of the
major reasons why there have been several
criticisms with regards to the state of poverty and
other sectorial development delays. To be more
explicit, when we consider the levels at which

---

[44] See Corruption and Development: The Fourth
Session of the Conference of the States Parties to the
United Nations Convention against Corruption in
Marrakech (24-28 October 2011). Available online at:
http://www.unodc.org/islamicrepublicofiran/en/impa
ct-of-corruption.html Retrieved on the 26th of May
2013.

corrupt (bribes) practices have been instituted within the sector of public works and public contracts, then we may realize that there is absolute need to fight this phenomenon at a 'degree higher than that of the global efforts to combat HIV/AIDS'. In a Friedrich-Ebert – Stiftung research report on corruption in Cameroon,[45] it attempts at previewing the stages at which corruption is carried out along the process of awarding government or public contracts thus:

1. **Placing of Purchase Order**. The corrupt practices begin at this stage where the vote holders circumvent the most controlled state procedures and statutory rules by breaking down the huge funds commitments into small lots that will grant them the latitude to do interpersonal agreements. Within this first stage the

[45] See Pierre TITI NWEL (1999).

report presents three levels at which the
corrupt practices are exhibited including:
the Call for Tenders in which though State
rules require that at least three candidates
be examined, a single candidate may apply
under three other fake names; the approval
as contractor or supplier in which the
aspiring supplier or contractor must dip his
hand into his pocket to be sure that the
vote holder will look favourably on him in
future; and the File for tenders in which
instead of the normal government charges
for physical stamps the candidate needs to
spend more in form of 'tips' in order for
documents to be duly and timely signed.

2. **The Award of Contracts**. In this stage,
the awarding commission needs to
examine all the bids before awarding a
contract but this is not the case because the
official rules are distorted in that, those

who have agreed to pay a bribe receive
information before hand on the maximum
prices and thus are able to propose the
lowest rates acceptable. Also, in
complicity with the vote holder, the
candidate may go in with several fictitious
company names in order to increase
his/her chances;

3. **The signing of the contract**. Here from
   the vote holder through the treasurer or
   accounts keeper to the other officials
   working under them, each gets to get a
   pinch from the candidate in order to
   facilitate the hectic procedural and
   discretionary undertakings under their
   departments;

4. **Implementation of the contract**. Here,
   for example like in a building contract,
   after receiving bribes, the civil engineers
   who of course by law are supposed, by the

end of the works, to attest that the
contractor follows all the technical
specifications prescribed, very often
simply gloss over all the technical
irregularities in their reports;

5. **Technical Reception and delivery of
   Supplies**. This level in which a technical
   reception committee needs to certify that
   the works had been carried out within the
   accepted standards of the contract before
   the procession to final payment, the
   contractor needs to dish out money in
   order to avoid bottlenecks or a last minute
   rejection; and

6. **Payment of Bills or Debit notes**. In this
   final stage for payment completion, before
   receiving payment, the supplier contractor
   must accept that 30% of the sum to be paid
   be deducted. This stage as reported is one
   of the most open stages through which

before payment of vouchers, the contractor needs a facilitator or a facilitating means to achieve his/her objective which is usually realized through preliminary agreements to be finalized at the moment of payment.

The situation is really very appalling, because assertively, one may realize that after all the in-route mini-deductions and major cuts taking off in the form of bribes within a single public works contract, the contractor may end up having only about 50 percent of the funds necessary to carry out the project. With this small amount, he/she will probably engage only about 25% to 30% of the said funds into the public works or worse still nothing at all since he/she has already paid for every official control procedure. As such, one can imagine the state and rate of development of a Cameroon facing this kind of crisis. In his research thesis to prove the hypothesis that

'*corrupt practices of public contract awarding
and payment issuance officers affect the planned
quality outputs of contractor's execution works*'
in Bamenda city of the North West Region of
Cameroon, NGYAH writes that:

> the securing process of public
> contracts which at times may
> entail the applicant public
> contractor to make percentage
> concessions to the public
> projects/contracts' awarding or
> selection committees and
> gladly offer overseers bribes
> which may dent the objectivity
> and accountability of the public
> works, is estimated 79.36%.
> Meanwhile, to make issues
> worse, the frequency level of
> payment issuance and field
> works inspection, delayed

payments and bribery which further frustrate public work plans, unscrupulous payments and ineffective field expectation is given at 73.02%, with the average effects of both angles at 76.19%. However, it is remarkably noticed that the highest level (79.36%) at which the quality of public contract work output is being devalued is at the very stage of its inception when those awarding the public contract start ripping-off the already budgeting funds through illegal commissions and other bribes.[46]

From NGYAH's analytical results, we can determine that, the actual output quality of a

---

[46] See NGYAH (2012b: 108)

corrupted public contract project implementation is given at 21.64% thus implying that virtually only one-fifth of the public contract funds (if any is used at all) is actually spend on the project activities meanwhile the rest is shared amongst the public contracts awarding and control officers and the public contractor's private interest. It a more expanded implication, this may mean that the country's growth or development rate is slowed down by five times at the level of the public contracts work domain.

Since the major goal of this paper is to see how some principal conflict driving factors may influence the Nation's great ambitions dream of 2035, the above results may imply that, instead of the becoming an emergent nation by 2035, if the current corruption statistical development impacts are not rigorously addressed, then the dream may only be realized by (35*5)—meaning in 2175. Though the nation has engage in some moderately acceptable measures at combating corruption which includes the creation of the national anti-corruption unit CONAC, the corruption phenomena still persist even in the midst of the country's growth and employment strategy 2010/2020 initiatives. According to the 2011 corruption report published by CONAC, excepts have already been highlighted within that writes thus:

> Many irregularities were discovered with the tendering for bids and award of contracts from feasibility studies to follow up of execution of the Lom-Pangar project. Cases of embezzlement of billions by members of the Cameroon civil service and managers of companies bidding for contracts were

discovered.—According to CONAC, the project has become very palatable to various wolves who have found an opportunity to enrich themselves from the sweat of Cameroon taxpayers. Instances of fraudulent payments made at the detriment of the State and corruption eating away public funds, which the State has to reimburse amounting to FCFA 2,054,717,180. (Two billions, fifty four million seven hundred thousand and one hundred and eighty).[47]

---

[47] See 2 Billions Embezzled from Lom-Pangar Project, CONAC publishes 2011 corruption report, 30 November 2012. Available online at: http://www.modernghana.com/news/433629/1/conac-publishes-2011-corruption-report.html retrieved on the 26th of May 2013.

Thus corruption is a major factor to the probable retardation and/or failure influence to be considered in the Cameroon's 2035 emerging nation dream.

A Brief Overview of Cameroon Growth and Employment Strategy Paper 2020

According to the President of the Republic's policy of "Greater Achievements", making up part of the long-term development vision (2035) in which the Government has undertaken to revise the economic growth and poverty reduction strategy, prepared as a Poverty Reduction Strategy Paper (PRSP) in consultation with the nation's development partners and IMF, the Growth and Employment Strategy Paper (GESP) 2010/2020 is part, covering the first ten years plan of action under the vision. Established to enhance the economic recovery of the country that started a decade ago, the Government prepared a Cameroon shared vision development paper to be fully implemented by 2035 that reads as follows: 'CAMEROON: AN EMERGING, DEMOCRATIC AND UNITED COUNTRY DESPITE ITS DIVERSITY'; and has four overall goals, namely: (i) reducing poverty to a socially acceptable level; (ii) becoming a medium-income country; (iii) acquiring the status of a Newly Industrialized Country; and (iv) reinforcing national unity and consolidating the democratic process.[48]

Since the principal focus of this study is to examine some of the available dispositions within GESP, and probably indicate some issues that need to be added or emphasized upon in order to attain and sustain the 2035 vision from an objectivist perspective rather than the already perceivable individualist anarchism spirit within the present model. The proposed review of the development policies, vision and goals, growth strategy, employment strategy, State governance and strategic management, and the institutional framework and monitoring mechanism of the implementation of the GESP are all wonderful in

---

[48] See International Monetary Fund (2010: 17)

their ambitious natures and categorically calculated for improved growth and wellbeing of the nations' 'economic macros and micros' but yet, I still find a profound emptiness in the whole rhetorical construe. Cameroon is not a nation that just appeared from nowhere, it is an institutionalized societal paradigm that went through 'thorns and thins' to become a full-fledged nation-State entity today and now aspiring upon highly ambitious national growth plans. The people of this nation have a history that is full of blood sacrifices and intense pain that began before its independence struggle and obtaining age through major political and socioeconomic structural changes that need full attention and address within the GESP.

Without a solid foundation, the house is bound to collapse during a strong wind and storm

From several analytical works carried out by national and global analysts, the peaceful stability of the country is at high risk.[49] At the beginning of this study, I took time out to highlight some of the uncountable instances that built grievances, some of which cumulated into violent clashes and others that were swallowed with such bitterness that the stances indigestible. It is true that, before any real major growth, there must be major scarifies, but at which extend and how do we contain the bitter outcomes of such sacrifices.

It is a good moment to repeat that a war is never won. Never mind that history books tell us the opposite. The psychological and material costs of war are so high that any triumph is a pyrrhic victory. Only peace can be won and winning peace means not only avoiding armed conflict but finding ways of eradicating the causes of individual and collective violence: injustice and oppression, ignorance

[49] See the International Crises group (2010)

and poverty, intolerance and discrimination. We must construct a new set of values and attitudes to replace the culture of war which, for centuries, has been influencing the course of civilization. Winning peace means the triumph of our pledge to establish, on a democratic basis, a new social framework of tolerance and generosity from which no one will feel excluded.[50]

In proceeding, I will be introducing the policy orientation stances within the GESP that actually need to be reviewed for the probable application of peace initiatives. This should serve as a consequential need from the already mentioned historical problems that the nation had faced

---

[50] See Federic Mayor. Peace Quotes. Available online at: http://www.wagingpeace.org/menu/issues/peace-&-war/start/peace-quotes/. Retrived on the 26th of May 2013

(outlined in the first section) — if proper measures
are not put in place to enhance any probable
recurrence, it may lead to very disastrous results to
the huge GESP investment scheme. In a later and
broader edition of this idea, to be contained in a
more extensive and detail national peace
implementation strategy manual proposal to
introduce and amend the GESP, I will therefore
include the national economy's sectorial policies to
be taken into consideration.

The Need for Institutional Peace Actualization
Stances within the GESP

The need for an actual and objectivist
consideration of introducing firm Peace initiatives
within the GESP runs from two major worries and
two major fears. 1). Do the Cameroonian people
actually care about or believe in this ambitious
policy that ought to be an idea worthy of a
celebration? 2). Has the government truly
considered the citizenry ideas upon this

development plan before instituting it? The two fears are: 1). In the advent of a major crises situation or a change of regime in the country, this great plan may cease its vibrant functionality zeal; 2). If the citizens do not regard the development process as of any beneficial importance to them, instead of protecting the investments, their humano-instinctual anarchist attitudes against the government may make them to engage in very destructive habits against investment structures. Addressing these worries for a recommendatory readjustment of the GESP will entail a brief historical analysis of the probable citizenry situations that has already been presented in the first section and the GESP policy lapses for the probable accommodation such opportunities.

Major Worry 1):   **Do the Cameroonian people actually care about or believe in this ambitious policy that ought to be an idea worthy of a celebration?**

This worry cuts across and also resolves the major fear (2). Briefly, from historical perspectives with regards to the severe economic crisis within an outcome in 1993 that made the State close to bankruptcy and was forced to slash civil service pay (salaries) by between 50 and 70 percent followed by a devaluation of the CFA franc in 1994, the Cameroonians still live in anger against the government because despite the fact that the economy recovered in the late 1990s, at least in terms of State finances, the victimized civil service personnel did not have any significant change to the regard but instead faced worsening situations. Also fostered by the fact that bribery, fraud and heavy embezzlements have become a habitual custom within all institutional milieus, the common and poor citizenry stay perpetually marginalized and discriminated upon. These are highly annoying issues within the society that build up grievances and grow distrusts and enmity against the State. The further question is, why would a persons who have watched major achievements occur severally within the nation but would not get a chance to benefit from any of such because of corruption, believe in such a vision when he/she already has a preconceived mind that the benefits are only for the 'rich' or highly connected. On the contrary, their antagonistic resentfulness against such development ideals may make them want to rather destroy the investments.

> Peace, in the sense of the absence
> of war, is of little value to
> someone who is dying of hunger
> or cold. It will not remove the
> pain of torture inflicted on a
> prisoner of conscience. It does not

comfort those who have lost their
loved ones in floods caused by
senseless deforestation in a
neighboring country. Peace can
only last where human rights are
respected, where people are fed,
and where individuals and nations
are free.[51]

As such we see that there is need to institute
national mechanisms within the GESP that could
slowly and progressively handle such phenomenal
understandings. Within the GESP's Executive
Summary point 3.3 Human Development
framework[52], much has been mentioned on
education but yet little or nothing has been
introduced with regards to a very vital human
development field as that of peace. Without a

---

[51] See The XIVth Dalai Lam. Peace Quotes. Available online
at: http://www.wagingpeace.org/menu/issues/peace-&-
war/start/peace-quotes/. Retrived on the 26th of May 2013

[52] See International Monetary Fund (2010: 20)

sound and considerable understanding of peace within the society, I believe all major development ventures are highly risky and probably wasteful ventures. Even at the level of national solidarity within the same section, it talks of reducing the dependency of vulnerable persons but yet still makes no mention on how these vulnerable persons would effectively accept their differences against the socially well-placed classes or contain their grievances against the obviously discriminatory society. In short, my idea here is that, this was supposed to institute and inscribe proper guideline measures at which every other developmental initiatives would be inclusive of a peace policy mechanism that is able to rebuild trust and citizen's believe systems for the nation's vision. This is because several past and present ongoing societal ill-packed experiences have instigated a loss of confidence in most if not all government initiatives. (measures would be more detailed in another proposal manual).

Major Worry 2): **Has the government truly considered the citizenry ideas upon this development plan before instituting it?**

This worry cuts across both major fears 1) and 2). Worries about historical and contemporary political conflicts pertaining to the citizenry aspirations need to be managed as a priority concern within any human development framework.

The goal toward which all history tends is peace, not peace through the medium of war, not peace through a process of universal intimidation, not peace through a program of mutual impoverishment, not peace by any means that leaves the world too weak or too frightened to go on fighting, but peace pure and simple based on that will to peace which has animated the overwhelming majority of mankind through countless ages. This will to peace does not arise out of a cowardly desire to preserve one's life and property, but out of conviction that the fullest development of the highest powers of men can be achieved only in a world of peace.[53]

Couple with the fact that the political situation of the country has lived extensive criticisms since the days of the people's popular request for a sovereign national conference in 1991 that led to severe strike actions and a 'ghost town' causing the lives of dozens of persons in the violent clashes between the activists and the

---

[53] Robert Maynard Hutchins (1899-1977). Peace Quotes. Available online at:
http://www.wagingpeace.org/menu/issues/peace-&-war/start/peace-quotes/. Retrieved on the 26th of May 2013

security forces, and also including serious confrontations on the university campus in Yaounde.[54] This was when the country first encountered the process of democratization and for the fact that since prehistoric period through the pre-colonial, colonial and post colonial era the indigenous autochthones have engraved much grieve, bitterness and anger against the administration, the fear that these people may become violent or violently retaliate in claims for vengeance and restoration is not to be considered imperceptibly. I believe that, because of the virtual peaceful nature of the country, the government has been taking for granted several measures upon insuring and building a more intensive and sustainable peace culture. It is understood that the several non-governmental organizations have been

---

[54] See footnote (48): Crisis Group interviews, participants in the events, Bafoussam and Douala, May 2009. See also "Soldiers return to Cameroon campus, strike shuts down Douala", Reuters, 19 April 1991. International Crises Group (2010).

carrying out several mini-structural adjustment
programs for sustaining the virtual peace in the
country but I dare to say that these initiatives are
not enough and do have very limited impact on the
virtual peaceful nature of the country. The duty of
keeping peace in the society is not based on
intervening only when there is an outbreak of a
conflict but is to strategize and institute national
mechanisms that would instill a true culture of
peace within the nation's citizenry (A detailed
frame work plan that I will be drawing up another
manual).

Following indicative elements of
institutional strength and weakness taken from
'Drivers of Fragility: What Makes a State Fragile?'[55]
In many respects, Cameroon is a classic fragile
State because on all measures, its institutions are
weak – low participation of the population in the

See – UK Department for International Development
working paper, London, 2005. International Crises Group
(2010: footnote 109)

political process, very problematic selection of political elites and little functioning oversight of government. This shows that, surely the citizenry aspirations were not taken into consideration before the institution of the GESP and as such the government really needs to worry about ideas of national peace and stability in an institutionalized manner because severe critical instances and probable violent conflicts may arise to this regard—public expenditure issues. In the GESP, paragraph 135 under article 2.2 of the development goals states that:

> In addition, through the objective of reinforcing national unity and consolidating the democratic process, the country seeks to reinforce the ideals of *peace*, freedom, justice, social progress, and national solidarity. The vision of unity implies reinforcing the

> sense of belonging to the same
> nation so that this becomes visible
> in individual and collective
> behaviour.[56]

Yet there is no single instant in the whole GESP that I see any tangible mechanism or ideal on how the peace aspects will be managed in a country like Cameroon that has been assessed to be a fragile State and vulnerable for a major civil conflict but chunks of lofty financial and material support for redressing temporary conflict situations. This is related to paragraph 424 of article 6.1.2 wherein a threat of the situation to the food security of the population and social peace promoted the riots of February 2008 and the Government is deciding to ensure a significant and rapid increase in the supply of agricultural produce by seeking to revive the production of rice in large plantations (Yagoua, Maga, Santchou, Ndop), develop the production of

---

[56] See International Monetary Fund (2010: 54)

corn and cassava in order to support the development of animal husbandry and poultry farming.[57] The former American President John F. Kennedy once said that:

> But peace does not rest in the charters and covenants alone. It lies in the hearts and minds of all people. So let us not rest all our hopes on parchment and on paper, let us strive to build peace, a desire for peace, a willingness to work for peace in the hearts and minds of all of our people. I believe that we can. I believe the problems of human destiny are not beyond the reach of human beings.[58]

---

[57] Ibid. 104

[58] See John F. Kennedy (1917-1963). Peace Quotes. Available online at:
http://www.wagingpeace.org/menu/issues/peace-&-

Therefore, peace is not an ideological consideration that because of its broadness should be excluded from plans with the hope that other collective solidarity endeavors would handle its goals. The society at large need to know what peace is all about and how to guide each other when faced with conflict situations and also how to control and maintain emotions within an objectivist spirit when our differences rise beyond certain levels.   The government needs to lay more emphasis on peace growth endeavours in all sectors of the economy.

Appreciating the GESP from its Fundamental Values

Form the definitional view of 'poverty' we notice that poverty does not only mean the lack of material issues but also a deficiency of more valued concerns such as 'emotions'.[59] Thus, given

---

war/start/peace-quotes/ Retrieved on the 26th of May 2013

[59] See Microsoft encartar dictionaries 2009.

that the GESP derives its fundamental base from the IMF's PRSP concept and that the government has been able to maintain a stable macroeconomic framework and sustain positive growth rates up to 2008 by implementing the PRSP adopted in April 2003 but still did not live up to the expected level necessary for drastic poverty reduction, the in-tuned notion of poverty reduction becomes an intriguing attribute that needs adequate analysis.

At high level macro-economic considerations, meanwhile in developed countries, notions of poverty are mostly upon structural failures, in developing nations, the issue of poverty is more profound due to the lack of government funds with a focus on social and political aspects that perpetuate poverty and, the perceptions of the poor has a significant impact on the design and execution of programs to alleviate poverty. The reasons, I believe, that the later is always failing is due to the fact that, most of these developing countries have not yet considered the real values of a nation's wealth. Of what use is all development and economic boost within a nation without upright and morally stable personalities to manage the boost for the benefit of all. 'The most common line of thought within the U.S. is that a person is poor because of personal traits.'[60] Citizens need to be firmly introduced and nurtured within proper ethical values of morals and peace. In Cameroon for example, the economic perception index has been on the rise for a while now but the country is said to be facing worse societal poverty levels especially within local communities. This is not the dream for the nation's greater ambition plan. The nation seeks to improve on the positive growth of moral, material and social standards of all its citizens and not just a particular group of persons.[61]

---

[60] See Rank, Mark R.; Yoon, Hong-Sik; Hirschl, Thomas A. (2003)

[61] See International Monetary Fund (2010: 54) paragraph 135

This group of persons which I mean here is in reference to the amoral hedonist and egocentric well placed government authorities who would rather see public money blocked-up in private close-ups than for a poor man to have two meals in a day. The nation needs to grow-up its citizenry in a conscience-stricken culture of mutual understanding and sharing that is worthy of 'self-contentment in small rather than a conscience-stricken guilt in much'. Cameroon's dream towards becoming and emerging nation therefore requires that it starts inculcating other cultural values that will enable it to arrive at such a stage. Stace Lindsay claims the differences between development-prone and development-resistant nations is attributed to mental models (which, like values, influence the decisions humans make).[62] Mental models are also cultural creations. Grondona, Harrison and Lindsay all feel that

---

[62] See Lindsay, Stace (2000).

without development orientated values and mindsets, nations will find it difficult if not impossible to develop efficiently, and that some sort of cultural change will be needed in these nations in order to reduce poverty. [63]

---

[63] See Harrison; Lindsay; Grodona (2000)

Conclusion

The nation of Cameroon is taking a very giant step forward through the President's recent 'greater ambition' policy discuss that is already in its manifestation phase within the growth and employment strategy paper 2010/2020 and an emerging nation policy plan to be realized by 2035. Yet as realistic as the great policy seems on its road to realization, it at the same pulls along the ambivalent dynamics that are fundamental prerequisites for such a development perspective and that have been posing intriguing worries upon the true political and cultural stability of such a macro-economic advancement measure meanwhile there are still severally pronounced worries upon the citizenry contentment and the country's sustainable peaceful stability as the present virtual peaceful spectrum proves. The 'emergence of a nation' is strongly bestowed on its human development capacity to deliver such emergent goals but if this human development aspect is not rightly targeted, then there is a problem.

'Where is the citizen's place in this huge development plan?'

Great economies are built to and for the service of men, thus, these men ought to be also mentally, morally and physical apt to effectively enjoy and sustain the fruits of such economies else they become futilitarian ventures prone to destruction and regression rather construction and progression.

Cameroon therefore needs to revise its human development construe within this plan in order to suite appropriate mental development goals that pull along basic moral ethic principles of the type of peace education that should be appropriate in promoting an automated self-responsive and mutual respect for the development ideas and structures and probably build in a sense of pride and belonging to such an ambitious nation.

By this, the government needs to institutionalize and invigorate an educational culture of peace and civics from a rudimentary level and up to the most advanced levels. Each Cameroonian should be able to consider his/her self as a learned peace maker then, from there on the national citizenry shall all in one way or the other be actively involved in building the 'nation of the dream'

References

Achille Mbembe(1996). *La naissance du maquis dans le Sud-Cameroun,1920-1960* (Paris, 1996).

Bouopda Pierre Kamé (2008). From Paul Biya's 2000 New Year's speech citation: *Les émeutes du renouveau Cameroun Février 2008* (Paris, 2008). Several Crisis Group interviews point to rapidly increasing levels of corruption from the early 1990s

Célestin Monga (2009). "L'argent qui appauvrit: un état des lieux macroéconomique et financier du Cameroun", in Fabien Eboussi Boulaga (ed.), *L'état du Cameroun 2008* (Yaoundé, 2009).

DeLancey, Mark W., and Mark Dike DeLancey (2000). *Historical Dictionary of the Republic of Cameroon* (3rd ed.). Lanham, Maryland: The Scarecrow Press.

Dominique Malaquais (2002). *Architecture, pouvoir et dissidence au Cameroun*, (Paris 2002).

Fabien Eboussi Boulaga (1997). *La Démocratie de transit au Cameroun* (Yaoundé, 1997).

Florence Charlier and Charles N'Cho- Oguie (2009). *Sustaining Reforms for Inclusive Growth in Cameroon*, World Bank (Washington, 2009).

Grondona, Mariano (2000). 'A cultural Typology of Economic Development', in Harrison, Lawrence E.; Huntington, Samuel P., *Culture Matters*, New York, NY: Basic Books, pp. 44–55.

Harrison, Lawrence E. (2000). 'Promoting Progressive Cultural Change', in Harrison, Lawrence E.; Huntington, Samuel P., *Culture Matters*, New York, NY: Basic Books, pp. 296–307

International Crisis Group (2010). *Cameroon: Fragile State? Crisis Group Africa* Report N°160, 25 May 2010.

International Monetary fund (2010).
Cameroon: Poverty Reduction Strategy Paper.
IMF Country Report No. 10/257

Jean-François Bayart (1978) 'The Political
System', in Richard Joseph (ed.), *Gaullist Africa:
Cameroon under Ahmadou Ahidjo* (Enugu, 1978).

Jean-François Bayart (1979)*., L'Etat au
Cameroun* (Paris, 1979)

Jean-François Médard (1978). 'L'État sous-
développé au Cameroun', *L'année africaine 1977*,
Paris, 1978.

**John Mukum Mbaku and Joseph Takougang
(eds.) (2004),** *The Leadership Challenge in Africa*
(Paris, 2004);

Joseph Takougang (1996). 'The 1992 Multi-party
Elections in Cameroon: Prospects for Democracy
and Democratization', *Journal of Asian and
African Studies*, 1996.

Kelly F. NGYAH (2012a). '*A functional Approach to the Digestion and Dissolution of Conflicts:* A structural Guide on Analysis, Negotiation, Management and Resolution Procedures towards Efficiently Handling Local and Global Conflicts' 1st ed. :MAHSRA &USIP

Kelly F. NGYAH (2012b). Corruption and Peaceful City Growth: *An Analysis To the Extend At Which Corruption within the Public And Private Sectors Hinders City Development and Peaceful Solidarity.* Case Study: Bamenda City In The Northwest Region Of Cameroon. Thesis Submitted To The Department Of Peace Studies, Cornerstone University & Theological Serminary Of Jerusalem – Isreal & USA. February 2012

Lindsay, Stace (2000). in Harrison, Lawrence E.; Huntington, Samuel P., *Culture Matters*, New York, NY: Basic Books, pp. 282–295.

M.W. Delancey (1987). 'The Construction of the Cameroon Political System: the Ahidjo Years

1958-1982', *Journal of Contemporary African Studies*, 1987

M. Terretta (2005). '"God of Independence, God of Peace": Village Politics and Nationalism in the Maquis of Cameroon, 1957-71', *Journal of African History*, 2005.

Milton Krieger (2008: chap 2). *Cameroon's Social Democratic Front: Its History and Prospects as an Opposition Party (1990-2011)* (Bamenda, 2008)

Nicodemus F. Awasom (1998). "Colonial Background to the Development of Autonomist Tendencies in Anglophone Cameroon, 1946-1961", *Journal of Third World Studies*, 1998

Peter Geschiere(1993). "Chiefs and Colonial Rule in Cameroon: Inventing Chieftaincy French and British Styles", *Africa*, 1993

Pierre TITI NWEL (1999). *Corruption in Cameroon.* GERDDES-Cameroon, FRIEDRICH-

EBERT –STIFTUNG. ISBN 2-911208-20-X
Available online at: http://library.fes.de/pdf-files/bueros/kamerun/07797.pdf Accessed on the 26th of may 2013.

Piet Konings and Francis Nyamnjoh (2003).
Negotiating an Anglophone Identity (Leiden, 2003).

Raju Singh (2013). *Cameroon Economic Update: Special Focus on Social Safety Nets.* The World Bank. Working for a World Free of Poverty. Available online at:
http://www.worldbank.org/en/news/feature/2013/01/29/cameroon-economic-update-special-focus-on-social-safety-nets Retrieved on the 24th of May 2013

Rank, Mark R.; Yoon, Hong-Sik; Hirschl, Thomas A. (2003). "American Poverty as a Structural Failing: Evidence and Arguments", *Journal of Sociaology and Social Welfare* **30** (4): 3–29.

Richard Joseph(1977). *Le mouvement nationaliste au Cameroun: les origines sociales de l'UPC (1946-1958)* (Paris, 1986, first published in 1977 as *The Radical Nationalist Movement in Cameroon*, but no longer in print in English),

Tiendi Joseph Ngalim (2006). Biya: *From Economic Failure to Modernity*. The Horizon No. 005 Yaounde, Cameroon. Tuesday 16th of May 2006. Pg. 4

Thobie et al. (1990). *Histoire de laFrance coloniale* (Paris, 1990)

Victor Julius Ngoh (1999). 'The Origin of the Marginalization of Former Southern Cameroonians (Anglophones), 1961-1966: An historical analysis', *Journal of Third World Studies*, 1999.

Victor T Le Vine(1964). *The Cameroons from Mandate to Independence* (Berkeley, 1964).

www.ingramcontent.com/pod-product-compliance
Lightning Source LLC
Chambersburg PA
CBHW022122280326
41933CB00007B/506